Anglican

Liturgical Identity

Papers from the Prague meeting of the International
Anglican Liturgical Consultation

edited by

Christopher Irvine

Contents

1. Introduction: Anglican Liturgical Identity *by Christopher Irvine*..... 3

2. Worship and Anglican Identity: a résumé *by Cynthia Botha*....... 12

3. Liturgy Unbound by the Book by *Trevor Lloyd*................. 20

4. 'Remembering the Future':
   Reflections on Liturgy and Ecclesiology *by Louis Weil*........... 31

Appendix: IALC-7 Prague discussion document: 'Liturgy and Anglican Identity'... 46

Copyright the respective contributors 2008

Contributors

Christopher Irvine is Canon Librarian at Canterbury Cathedral, and is a consultant to the Church of England's Liturgical Commission. He is the author of *The Art of God: the making of Christians and the meaning of worship* (SPCK, 2005), and has recently edited *The Use of Symbols in Worship* (SPCK, 2007).

Cynthia Botha is a priest of the Anglican Church of Southern Africa (diocese of Johannesburg). She is the Convenor of its Liturgical Committee and Secretary to the Province's Media and Publications Committee.

Trevor Lloyd, formerly Archdeacon of Barnstaple, was a member of the Church of England's Liturgical Commission, and has written extensively on liturgical matters. He is one of the editors of *Connecting with Baptism: A Practical Guide to Christian Initiation* (Church House Publishing, 2007).

Louis Weil is the James F. Hodges and Harold and Rita Haynes Professor of Liturgics at the Church Divinity School of the Pacific, California, USA, and his recent publications include *The Theology of Worship* (Cowley Publications, 2001).

The Cover Picture
Is a photo of the Compass Rose, symbol of the Anglican Communion, as exemplified on both frontal and floor at Canterbury Cathedral, and is published by permission

First impression June 2008
ISSN 0951-2667
ISBN 978-1-85311-914-9

1. Introduction: Anglican Liturgical Identity
By Christopher Irvine

'where it is in error, correct it...where it is in want, furnish it; where it is divided, heal it, and unite it in thy love.' Archbishop William Laud (1573-1645).

The question of what might hold the autonomous Churches of the Anglican Communion together is a topical and pressing question as this Study is published, just before bishops from around the globe gather for the Lambeth Conference in July 2008 in the hope of rediscovering their sense of a shared Anglican identity. But what precisely is it that constitutes this, historically speaking, modern sense of belonging together? Are there recognizable identifying characteristics, or a particular culture and ethos which we can confidently categorize as being 'Anglican'?

We have recently seen a spate of writing on the subject of Anglican identity [1], and since Bishop Stephen Sykes's seminal work in preparation for the 1978 Lambeth Conference[2], the theological and the political complexion of Anglicanism has shifted and become increasingly polarized over issues of polity, doctrine and order. The once favoured value of 'comprehension' has been overridden by personal and sectarian conviction. However unwelcome this may be, perhaps we should not be too surprised to see the situation in the Communion mirroring the wider socio-economic conditions of globalization, where the ubiquity of universal branding merely masks an increasingly divided and competitive social world. Further, the ambivalent legacy of 19th century colonial missionary activity should make us wary of advocating a definitive Anglican brand, and a little more sensitive to a shared history, which was and is experienced and interpreted in different ways. In looking to the wider picture, we must also reckon with those Anglican provinces and national churches, such as Nippon Sei Ko Kai

---

[1] Rowan Williams, *Anglican Identities* (DLT, London, 2004), Colin Podmore, *Aspects of Anglican Identity*, (Church House Publishing, London, 2004), Colin Buchanan, *Historical Dictionary of Anglicanism* (Scarecrow, Maryland, USA, 2006), Paul Avis, *The Identity of Anglicanism: Essentials of Anglican Ecclesiology* (T&T Clark, Edinburgh, 2008). For liturgical issues across the Communion see Charles Hefling and Cynthia Shattuck (eds), *The Oxford Guide to the Book of Common Prayer: A Worldwide Survey* (Oxford University Press, New York, 2006)

[2] Stephen Sykes, *The Integrity of Anglicanism* (Mowbrays, London and Oxford, 1978).

(Holy Catholic Church of Japan), and the Anglican Church of Mexico, which are not a part of the British colonial legacy, and do not trace their origins directly back to the Church of England. In these cases, we might ask what these ecclesial communities were 'buying into' when they became a part of the Anglican Communion. This question returns us again to the issue of Anglican identity. Historically, the key characteristics of the Provincial ecclesial polity which, along with a foundational affirmation of communion with Canterbury, marks Anglicanism is a triumvirate: the three-fold order of bishop, priest and deacon, the principal authority of scripture, and liturgical (ordered) worship, and, as these three features coalesce in the context of worship, Anglican liturgy clearly functions as a highly significant index of Anglican identity.

International Anglican Liturgical Consultations (IALC) have been convened at two- or four-year intervals since 1985.[3] IALC-7 in Prague in 2005 addressed this question of Anglican liturgical identity. This Study presents an expansion, for which I, as editor, am responsible, of a preparatory paper for the Consultation written by Cynthia Botha. There follow two keynote papers given at the Consultation by Trevor Lloyd and Louis Weil, and in conclusion the discussion paper from the Consultation.[4] The title 'discussion paper' is important because those who contributed to the discussion recognized that what had been drafted was an invitation to further work on the topic (hence the inclusion of questions at the end of the document) rather than a definitive statement. Such modesty resulted not only from a shared feeling that the meeting was not fully representative of the Communion, but that the topic itself was an elusive one. The very term 'identity' is a loaded word and is a very slippery concept to work with, let alone to elucidate and think through in any sustained systematic way. The predictable starting point for our deliberations at Prague was the question of uniformity, and the use of Prayer Books in worship.

---

[3] The story of the IALCs is told in David Holeton and Colin Buchanan, *A History of the International Anglican Liturgical Consultations 1983-2007* (Joint Liturgical Study no.63, 2007).
[4] The uneven composition of the meeting and the process whereby the 'discussion paper' was produced are reported in Joint Liturgical Study no.63; but the Study calls it a 'statement'; and, as one of the editors of the paper, I should make it clear here that it was a 'discussion paper' and not a 'statement', though the error was also found in the 2006 new year edition of *Anglican World* no.120.

Introduction

The confident assertion of the 1908 Lambeth Conference, that the Book of Common Prayer was the benchmark of Anglican faith and practice[5], was recast forty years later in terms of a recognition of the book as a bond of unity holding the Communion together. [6] This idealization of the unifying role of the Prayer Book was predicated on the principle of uniformity (a discussion of which I have expanded in Cynthia Botha's essay), and it is difficult to square it with the historic fact that the Churches of the Anglican Communion, since the 17th century have in reality worked with a series of English Prayer Books as diverse from 1662 as the 1549 and the 1637 books. As we map, both historically and geographically, the authorized liturgical usage around the Communion, the use of a single book emerges as a matter of ideology rather than a description of actual practice. Although such practice did vary slightly around the Communion by the end of the 19th century, nevertheless the bishops at Lambeth in 1908 appear to have affirmed 'the Book of Common Prayer' as a bond of the Communion without any sense of ambiguity about exactly which book was meant.

For many, of course, the 1662 Book took precedence and was given pride of place, although as early as Lambeth 1948 it was conceded that uniformity, in the sense of everyone having to use the same book, was not necessary as long as Anglican worship and doctrine were compatible with it. The decisive impetus for the provinces of the Communion to engage in provincial liturgical revision and renewal was given by the Lambeth Conference of 1958, albeit in rather cautious terms. In addition, although Cranmer's statement that every country should use such ceremonies as they considered best to the setting forth of God's honour and glory was a claim to legitimize England's independence from Rome, it has been the basis upon which the freedom of individual provinces and churches in communion with the see of Canterbury was laid, a freedom to shape worship in accordance with their particular cultural forms. This process was given particular momentum by the view of provincial juridical autonomy within the Anglican Communion, increasingly recognized and affirmed by successive Lambeth

---

[5] Resolution 36, Lambeth Conference 1908
[6] Resolution 78a, Lambeth Conference, 1948

Conferences since 1878, when the need to tolerate diversity within the Communion was first articulated. Article 34 of the 39 Articles of 1571 appears to give full licence to a national Church to change its liturgical forms, and points the way towards the casting of worship in the cultural forms of language and customs, music and vesture, belonging to an indigenous people. But it was not until the Lambeth 1988 that inculturation, as such, was endorsed. Even then a condition was attached that any cultural adaptation had to follow 'agreed Anglican norms' of prayer. What these Anglican norms might be remains an open question, and one which I intend to nudge forward in this Introduction.

Although our foundation documents are susceptible of different interpretations, the prevailing trend has been an intentional way of Christian life which accords with scripture and is consistent with the belief and practice of the 'undivided, primitive Church', not rigidly cast in confessional statements, but in the form of common prayer which is understood by the people. Hence the received wisdom was that, if you wanted to know what Anglicans believed, you needed to participate in their worship. Whether such a generalized principle still holds in our contemporary context of diversity is a real question. It could be argued that the diverse styles of worship within, as much as between, provinces has long eroded a recognizable commonality in Anglican worship. The feverish flurry of liturgical revision during the final decades of the 20th and into the 21st century, monitored and to some extent orchestrated by the IALC as it related to the Anglican Consultative Council, was accelerated by increasing ecumenical convergence, and the production of agreed English liturgical texts, most notably by the International Consultation on English Texts, and its later form, the English Language Liturgical Consultation. In addition, reference should be made to the compilation and widespread adoption of the Revised Common Lectionary, which set the pattern of scripture readings for the Christian year for a number of provinces.

Introduction

There is, of course, a shared history but not necessarily a common memory. The stories of our origins are told differently, and tell of significant differences, and yet a shared DNA, a shared set of inherited identifying characteristics, might well emerge as we listen to each others' stories across the Communion. Focusing on core texts, common individual prayers, such as Cranmer's rendering of the collect for purity, his composite prayer of humble access, or on particular genres of prayer, such as the litany, might be like searching for a missing gene, but identifying a common DNA might yet be possible.

One key characteristic might be the emphasis upon word and sacrament. Historically, the two elements have jostled for supremacy, and it would be too idealistic to posit an equal balance between word and sacrament. Nevertheless, the twin foci of worship in word and sacrament reflect the 'reformed' and 'catholic' features of the history of Anglican Reformations, and were asserted as the condition upon which Lambeth 1958 approved liturgical revision across the provinces and churches of the Communion. Today some contemporary and extraneous influences, such as styles of worship inspired by the Vineyard model, in which sustained public reading of scripture is replaced by worship songs and sacramental expression is eclipsed by the desire for immediate individual religious experience, exacerbate the difficulty of maintaining a balance of word and sacrament in contemporary worship.

Liturgically, we live in a mixed economy, and one which values and actively promotes variety, flexibility and local enrichment, but this does not lead inevitably to the displacement of the central place of the Bible, font, and the table of the Lord. On the contrary, as Christian discipleship deepens it seems to require a more sustaining scriptural diet and sacramental sensibility.

It could be said that what has been enunciated here is common across all liturgical traditions, both East and West, Catholic, Orthodox and Reformed, but perhaps we could extend the analogy of DNA and offer a fuller sketch of some Anglican characteristics. These could be read as being *core principles*, or, to use a less loaded expression, tendencies, which belong as much to history as well as being possible points of reference whereby we might chart future developments:

1. Worship is *liturgical* and has an ordered shape and common structure. Lambeth 1978 endorsed the view that a unity of *structure* could happily be combined with a greater flexibility in the content of common prayer, a view which attracted ecumenical consensus and was developed in the IALC documents of the Toronto (1991) and Dublin (1995) Consultations on Baptism and Eucharist respectively [7]. Against this focus on *structure* one might also observe that words, or the content are equally significant, as the story of the revisions of English Prayer Book testifies [8]. The often cited principle of lex *orandi, lex credendi* (as we worship, so we believe), is reciprocal and works in both directions, with our belief being shaped by our praying together, and by authorized forms of worship being shaped by the doctrinal understandings and perspectives of those who compose and authorize them. The vocabulary of the Church's prayer, we could say, has a grammar of doctrine.

2. Worship is essentially corporate and envisages a wider social intentionality and bearing. What is recognized here is that those who consciously enter the presence of God are implicated in networks of social relationships set by the claims of our neighbour and of divine justice. It is sometimes wryly observed that the 'collection' is the ritual high point of a Church of England service,

---

[7] Re baptism see David R.Holeton (ed), *Growing in Newness of Life: Christian Initiation in Anglicanism Today* (Anglican Book Centre, Toronto, 1993) pp.252-253. Re the eucharist the structure described is: 1. Gathering, 2. Proclaiming and Receiving the Word of God, 3. Prayers of the People, 4. Celebrating at the Lord's Table, and 5. Going out as God's People (see David R.Holeton (ed), *Our Thanks and Praise: The Eucharist in Anglicanism Today* (ABC, Toronto, 1998) p.284). The favouring of structure in liturgical studies can be traced back to an article by Robert Taft in which he appropriates the critical tools of structural analysis. See R.Taft 'The Structural Analysis of Liturgical Units: An Essay in Methodology' in *Worship* 52 (1978).

[8] A case in point is the doctrine of consecration that emerged in the 1662 book and cannot be retrospectively predicated of Cranmer's 1552 rite.

but its origins in Cranmer's introduction of 'the poor men's box' speaks of a deliberate welding together of our being called to divine service and the obligation placed upon the Christian community to provide for those in need. For us, this dual accent on social responsibility and corporate/common prayer contrasts with any inward-turned group of like-minded individuals, and, at the other extreme, the anonymity of mega-churches. Again, the corporate character of worship underlines how liturgy is dialogical, with ordained and lay people together voicing the Church's prayer and praise through the classic structure of versicles and responses, reading and canticles. In essence, this is Cranmer's vision of the Church, with the structure of catholic order, and of the whole people of God gathered together in prayer and praise under the word, and around the Lord's table.

3. The Bible is central and is to be read in the vernacular according to a lectionary system to ensure the reading of the full sweep of biblical literature. Cranmer's evident intention was to facilitate a greater biblical literacy among Christian people. Furthermore, scripture is to be *heard* (which means more than simply a public reading) in the context of shared worship.[9] The primacy of the liturgical setting for the hearing of scripture guards against individual interpretations of the Bible, and suggests a particular liturgical hermeneutic. The hearing and reception of the word in the setting of corporate worship, as distinct from a private reading, was amplified by the architect of Anglican polity, Richard Hooker, who stressed how the Bible was heard as scripture when it was read aloud as part of divine service [10], and introduced the idea that the reading of the Bible in worship was also doxological, a service performed *to* God, as well as for the edification of those who heard it read.

---

[9] Both 1552 and 1662 Prayer Books direct the curate to toll the bell 'that the people may come to hear God's word and pray with him.' What Cranmer envisaged was the kind of corporate Office which later was given classic Anglican expression by George Herbert. His poem *Aaron* concludes with the words 'Come people; Aaron's drest.'

[10] This point is explicitly made by Cranmer in the preface to the first vernacular Prayer Book where he speaks of the 'daily hearing of scripture in holy assembly.' For Hooker, see *Laws of Ecclesiastical Polity*, Book V. IX. 1-5.

Other features of Anglican worship, though potentially of equal importance and to a greater or lesser extent paralleled in other liturgical traditions, can be stated in a more summary form:

- The coming together of a congregation is the occasion for a corporate confession, a public confession of sins and absolution. Cranmer evidently held that the minister had 'authority' to declare God's forgiveness, and in his service for the Visitation of the Sick, retained the traditional priestly formula: 'I absolve thee from all thy synnes'.

- The patterns of our common prayer are inextricably bound up with ecclesiology, especially episcopacy. The diocesan bishop is the chief liturgical minister, and ordained ministers exercise a local and delegated sacramental and teaching ministry under the bishop. It was this firm ecclesiological stamp upon worship that led Lambeth 1978 to argue that our unity as Anglicans was grounded not in the use of a common book, but of our being a local manifestation of the 'One, Holy, Catholic and Apostolic Church.' [11]

- Anglicans subscribe to a single baptism in the three-fold name of the Trinity, and regard baptism and the eucharist as the defining moments in Christian identity and ecclesial belonging.

- Anglican worship has an aesthetic sensibility. It promotes a quality of language in worship, deploys local arts and music in its setting, and is committed to performing worship well, 'decently and in order'.

- It marks time through a calendar of the Christian Year and is committed to the practice of daily prayer.

- Anglicans value the Psalms as a key element in daily prayer, and since the time of Cranmer have made provision for, and have used, a liturgical Psalter.

- Acts of worship regularly conclude with a blessing of the congregation as the formal end of the service.

---

[11] See *The Lambeth Conference 1978*, p. 79.

These principles are neither prescriptive, nor intended as a check-list to exclude, but an attempt to map out some general defining qualities. They are not ranked in order of importance, or as having an equal weighting of importance. Some will attract a greater degree of recognition and consensus than others, but each will have some resonance with present and inherited patterns of authorized common prayer for all across our global Communion.

In the final analysis it might not be wise to posit a single Anglican identity, but rather to speak of 'Anglican identities', particular shared features which in any one case may be heightened or lost, and indeed, ranked differently as historic and social circumstances change. It has been observed that character emerges over time [12], and perhaps identity too results from the vicissitudes of history, and only emerges in recognizable form after a period of deliberate reflection on past experience. Our hope is that whatever we might detail as Anglican liturgical identity, a period of shared and prayerful reflection on the part of all those within the Anglican Communion on what it means to be Anglican will show a sufficiently robust 'character' to hold together in tension the provinces and churches of the world-wide Anglican Communion, so that it may effectively witness both to the reciprocal relationships of those who belong to 'one world', and to the divine purpose that the kingdoms of this world will become the kingdom of our God and of his Christ.

---

[12] Kenneth Stevenson and Bryan Spinks (eds), *The Identity of Anglican Worship* (Mowbray, 1991) p.x.

2. Worship and Anglican Identity - a Résumé
Cynthia Botha

So what is it that makes worship, Anglican worship? Take, for example, the opening eucharist at a recent provincial Synod in Southern Africa. There was a borrowing of texts from other sources and it acknowledged material from other provinces, principally the New Zealand Prayer Book (1989) and the new Church of Ireland's *Book of Common Prayer* (2004). There was very little material from *An Anglican Prayer Book* (1989), the Prayer Book of our province. This elicited a number of comments and some people at the Synod were dismayed by the absence of local contextualized material. Disappointment was also expressed at the fact that the service was largely in English, with the various vernacular languages used within the province being largely restricted to the hymns and scripture readings.

Reflecting on this experience, I wonder if it would be replicated across the provinces in the Anglican Communion, and the impression given by the range of preparatory papers circulated to those who attended the Prague IALC would suggest that the 'borrowing' of liturgical texts from the official provision of other provinces is a fairly widespread practice. So we in Southern Africa are not alone! In fact, the New Zealand preparatory paper written by George Connor admitted that a considerable freedom has been allowed there in borrowing liturgical material from a range of sources, specific examples including collects from *A Prayer Book For Australia* (1995), prayers over the gifts and post-communion prayers from the Canadian *Book of Alternative Services* (1985), and introductions to the prayers of penitence and the Peace from the Church of England's *Common Worship.* Stipulation is made that, on occasions when the eucharist is celebrated, then only an authorized Great Thanksgiving (eucharistic prayer) is to be used. Nevertheless, the borrowing of liturgical material from other provinces is evidently widespread in New Zealand, which affords an even greater freedom through the provision of a skeletal structure consisting of an authorized three-fold worship template of 'Gather', 'Story' and 'Go'.

A similar scenario was presented by Jean Cambell OSH, who, writing from an American context, described a eucharist in her preparatory paper which included a eucharistic prayer from New Zealand, and music and songs from the ecumenical Iona Community in Scotland and the American Roman Catholic Hymnal. Although The Episcopal Church (USA) retains its 1979 Prayer Book, Sr. Jean commented on how the 20th century had seen greater diversity in liturgical practice than at any other time in its history. The 1979 Prayer Book, she argued, opened up the potential for greater diversity and allowed for example, within the eucharist, a series of categories for the prayers of the people so that they could formulate their own prayers or use one of the six forms provided. Further variations in the shaping of worship are provided in *Enriching our Worship, Volume 1* (1997)

The scope of available liturgical sources, both official and unofficial, has broadened beyond imagining for those with the computer technology to access and download from the worldwide web. Paul Bradshaw, writing from an English context, drew attention to the way in which downloaded texts are sometimes combined with visual images and projected onto a screen, but how far the adoption of this passive 21st century screen culture in freeing people from the book liberates them to be more engaged in worship, is a debatable point.

Such whole-scale borrowing and potentially infinite combinations of alternatives and sources for liturgical and musical texts effectively undermines even the semblance of uniformity.

The Anglican legacy of Uniformity is rooted in the English break from the Church in Rome during the reign of Henry VIII and, after the accession of Edward VI, in the considerable shift in popular religious culture that was enforced 'top-down' by the 1549 Act of Uniformity to bring in the first Book of Common Prayer and ensure 'one usage in this realm of England'. This in turn provided Thomas Cranmer with the opportunity to press towards a more radical reform in the second English Prayer Book of 1552. A hiatus followed Edward's brief reign, and a new Act of Uniformity came to the statute book under Elizabeth I. A single liturgical usage in the vernacular language was enshrined in the minutely revised Book of Common Prayer of 1559.

These slight modifications amounted to virtually no doctrinal change; but the liturgical battle-ground had now changed. In Edward's reign it had been orientated chiefly against Roman Catholicism (though that remained an issue in Elizabeth's day, particularly in light of the Council of Trent and of the Pope's excommunication of her and denunciation of her legitimacy as monarch). But the Elizabethan Church found itself domestically far more in conflict with Puritan ideals for public worship, and its 'uniformity' was therefore defensive, rather than revolutionary as it had been in Cranmer's day.

In practice the Elizabethan Settlement, despite the apparent straitjacket of the Act of Uniformity, allowed a degree of diversity. The Royal Injunctions of 1559 even gave official sanction for what many would today reckon to be a telling feature of Anglican worship, the singing of hymns and the choral tradition: '...for the comforting of such as delight in music, it may be permitted, that at the beginning, or in the end of common prayers, either at morning or at evening, there may be sung an hymn, or suchlike song to the praise of Almighty God in the best sort of melody and music that may be conveniently devised.'[13] But if we pursue the question as to who might devise such music and provide the lyrics, we see that this Injunction opened the gates to local choice and resources. Colin Buchanan has observed that this Elizabethan Injunction opened the way for both the 18th century Evangelical Revival, and the 19th century Catholic Revival, as both movements relied heavily on popular hymnody to popularize their respective pieties and doctrines.[14]

In English Church life, the Prayer Book might have provided a single script, and 1662 certainly appeared to reinforce that. However, over the years, and particularly with the coming of the anglo-catholic movement in the 19th century, the variety of ways in which it was staged and performed rather gave the lie to the myth of strict uniformity. The most decisive shift in actual official texts towards greater variation and local adaptation came with the publication of the *Alternative Service Book* of 1980.

---

[13] Royal Injunction XLIX

[14] The source is Colin Buchanan's paper on 'Liturgical Uniformity', published in the Australian *Journal of Anglican Studies* (December 2004), and circulated as an offprint to be a Prague preparatory paper.

The direction that the president at the eucharist '*may use these, or other suitable words*' occurs in five key places in the rite. But perhaps the final unravelling of uniformity was presaged by *Patterns for Worship* (1995), and reached its full form in *Common Worship* 'A Service of the Word'. Bradshaw describes it in these terms: 'The "Service of the Word" is not a service as such but simply a minimum framework to which any form of service must adhere in order to be recognized as Anglican. All that it requires is that the confession, absolution, the collect and creed or other affirmation of faith must follow authorized texts, and that there should be reading from scripture and the Lord's Prayer.'[15] Perhaps this liturgical provision spells the death-knell of the historic aspiration for liturgical uniformity in England.

Globally, however, there are rare exceptions where a fidelity to both the rubrics and the text of the 1662 Prayer Book is a result of earlier missionary activity. Writing from Kenya, Joyce Karuri speaks of the local translations of the Book of Common Prayer in Kenya being so faithful to the structure that it was a total replica of the BCP. Even the breakaway churches use this prayer book and hymnbook – something she sees as arising out of an absence of serious scholarship in these churches. In more recent times the growing influence and popularity of Pentecostal churches, a significant number of which are financially supported by mega-Charismatic churches in the United States, have led Joyce Karuri to express the view that authentic liturgical development depends upon a fidelity to inherited Anglican forms of service: Liturgical maturity in Kenya, she has written, may never quite be realized as long as successive church leaders neglect to build on the foundations laid by their predecessors. It is undoubtedly the case that there was little variation from 1662 in the Prayer Book revisions of a number of provinces around the Anglican Communion during the first half of the 20th century. Changes that were made, such as in Canada in 1922, were conservative and modest.

---

[15] Paul Bradshaw ' "All the whole realm shall have but one use": Reflections on Liturgical Uniformity in the Church of England' (Prague preparatory paper).

The preparatory papers circulated to members of IALC before the Prague meeting, which have been extensively drawn into this résumé, did not present the whole global picture, as there was little from Africa, and nothing from the Indian subcontinent, or Asia.. But the papers that were written focused on the question of uniformity. From a historic perspective, it could be argued, as Christopher Irvine has suggested in chapter 1, that, for Cranmer, uniformity was a means to an end, a legal mechanism to deliver the more significant aim of his religious reforms, namely a vernacular liturgy understood by the people. Further, Cranmer's project was arguably as much social as religious in seeking to unify the English people through the use of one book. In this sense, as Cranmer seems to admit, the project is geographically bound and only concerned the English people, for as Cranmer said: '... in these our doinges, we condemne no other nacions, nor prescribe any thing, but to our owne people only.'[16]

Today the growing multicultural and linguistic needs of people around the worldwide Anglican Communion need to be recognized and accommodated, and this is a considerable and complex challenge. New Zealand offers us an interesting insight into how translation may be effectively done. George Connor writes, 'In the 1989 New Zealand Prayer Book the translation adopts a Maori language style closer to normal Maori idioms and phraseology and some services were first prepared in Maori and then translated into English. An additional Eucharist solely in Maori was also included which incorporates more traditional language within a carefully thought out and culturally appropriate structure. Most experimentation relates to non-eucharistic services.'[17] In other words whilst the eucharist was retained in its traditional format, thus allowing people to continue to worship within the familiar structure, space was also made for cultural adaptation which also provided continuity. This could be a way forward for us in some parts of the Anglican Communion, as we try to accommodate inculturation and multi-lingual expression whilst retaining the familiar pattern and flow of the service.

---

[16] 'Of Ceremonies, why some be abolished, and some retained.' (Second Prayer-Book of Edward VI, 1552)
[17] George Connor, 'Liturgical Uniformity versus Local freedom' (Prague preparatory paper).

While researching the background to the *South African Prayer Book*, I discovered that even as early as the late 1800s some bishops required their clergy to learn the local language of the people amongst whom they ministered. And so translation of the BCP into the local African languages started at a very early stage. More recently the English-language edition of *An Anglican Prayer Book* 1989 was used as the text from which the translation into some nine vernacular languages has, at the time of writing, been completed. Every effort was made to ensure that page numbers and marginal numbers were exactly the same. This gave rise to a uniform text which is seen by some as rather conservative, but it does assist parishes where often more than one language is used at any one service.

Translation, of course, is only one element in the complex task of inculturation, of using the riches of our diverse cultural and linguistic communities, which is now on the agenda. Our Southern Africa Synod has affirmed its support for the right of a diocesan bishop to authorize culturally appropriate forms of service with the proviso that they are consistent with the doctrines and discipline of the Church. Yet, despite this encouragement regarding the importance of inculturation, it is still not pursued in some parts of the Communion as vigorously as it might be.[18]

In Southern Africa the special Commission set up to look at inculturation of the liturgy was neither very active nor very successful. In some instances, this is because of a lack of resources in the poorer parts of our province. I am aware, for instance, of how missionary endeavours in Angola and Mozambique have made translations of the Prayer Book a priority, but the lack of financial resources has frustrated the project. Bishop Dinis Sengulane from Mozambique has recently expressed his concerns with me about the lack of current expertise and resources available to help African Anglicans find appropriate

---

[18] IALC-3 at York in 1989 tackled inculturation, and, expounding two resolutions of Lambeth 1988, produced a statement 'Down to Earth Worship'. This is published with supporting essays in David R.Holeton (ed), *Liturgical Inculturation in the Anglican Communion* (Joint Liturgical Study no.15, Grove Books, 1990).

expressions in developing liturgies that are dynamic and applicable to local contexts, or, as he phrased it, 'a skeleton around which flesh is to be provided locally'.

This request for a 'skeleton' liturgy connects with the emerging consensus, underlined in the IALC preparatory papers, of the significance of 'structure'. The point was well articulated by Paul Gibson who spoke of an appropriate liturgical pattern, and argued that what he proposed was not an 'ur' structure which should be followed everywhere, but a sense of the liturgy as an unfolding sequence of events. Models of liturgical structure are already available in some provinces of the Anglican Communion. We have already mentioned the template of 'Gather', 'Story', 'Go' in New Zealand, to which we should add the 'Outline Eucharist' in the American 1979 provision, the Canadian 'Order for the Eucharist', and the Church of England's 'Service of the Word'. The Church of England has further required that the texts of the confession, absolution, the collect and creed (or affirmation of faith) should follow authorized texts. In Southern Africa the 'Service of the Word' has been discussed and submitted for approval to the Synod of Bishops. These models provide a framework to which any form of service must adhere to be recognized as Anglican. And so, as observed in the Introduction, we might infer that it is now structure, shape and pattern, which have emerged as the effective hallmark of Anglican liturgical identity.

We have already remarked on one aspect of increasing diversity in worship, and that is the variety of hymns and worship songs used around the Communion, particularly in America, New Zealand and Britain. In South Africa hymns are often sung simultaneously in different languages to the same tune, but announced according to their number in different hymnals: hymn no.123 in *Ancient and Modern*, no. 456 in Setswana, no. 789 in isiXhosa, and so on, which results in a most compelling blend of sound and music. The real point at issue is the sheer variety of worship songs and hymns. When one reflects on the fact that most of what worshippers come to believe is conveyed through song, the question arises as to whether hymn books and worship songs should receive the same degree of synodical and episcopal scrutiny as liturgical texts. As previously remarked, the technological revolution has made an infinite number of worship texts, hymns and worship songs immediately available through the worldwideweb. The internet is a means of globalization, and what is accessed might not only be detrimental to local contexts, but might promote expressions of religious belief and devotion which are at variance with even the broad styles and emphases of Anglican worship. In South Africa, these concerns have led our Church to ask the bishops to remind clergy that texts downloaded from the internet are not authorized for use. But even if this practice, which is by no means restricted to South Africa, could be policed, is it something that we could, or would, want to do?

An equally pressing concern to emerge from our preparatory papers is the apparently increasing lack of adequate liturgical knowledge and skill among those responsible for planning worship. This is an increasing challenge facing all of us across the Communion. How is liturgical education and formation to be adequately resourced in each Province, and how is the liturgical work to be more effectively coordinated across the Communion? It is vital that our programmes of lay and clergy training provide opportunities for liturgical formation and education, for those who shape our liturgy require insight and skill to make wise choices in the use of diverse liturgical resources. They also need to be sensitive to what is appropriate in the local context, and at the same time should be mindful of the traditions of Anglican spirituality and doctrine.

In conclusion then, even in a world of globalization, I believe that there can be no uniformity and thus no uniform expression of worship. Ultimately, worship is an expression of our being invited to share the life of God the Holy Trinity, and to be in solidarity with those who seek the transformation of the world according to God's justice, and the renewal of all creation. It therefore must and will always be dynamic. Whatever its form, worship will always need to express the truth of God's love made manifest to us through the power of the Spirit in the life, death, resurrection and continuing presence of Jesus in our midst.

3. Liturgy Unbound by the Book
Trevor Lloyd

This title 'Liturgy unbound by the book' invites us to examine the question as to how those cultures which either have never had, or have moved away from, the regular use of books in worship, fit in with a tradition that has in the past largely defined itself in terms of a book. What can we learn for our present exercise from such cultures? Have they abandoned traditional Anglicanism or simply moved to redefine it in some way? There are clearly a number of different categories

1. Places where books are not used because the technology is lacking or books are too expensive, and so Anglican worship happens without printed texts. There are undoubtedly places within the Communion where this is so, and where books are hard to come by because of decay or infestation. One thinks of the protestant termites in Madagascar putting an end to reservation by consuming the sacrament: books no doubt can suffer the same fate, or Readers in Uganda learning Morning and Evening Prayer by heart in order to lead worship.

2. A sub-category of this is where, as in medieval England, only the priest has a book, and the congregation observe or join in with responses they know by heart, or are taught line by line by the minister. I spoke recently to a priest from the Solomon Islands, who said the priest would have a book for the eucharist, but the congregation would know everything by heart, including their repertoire of hundreds of hymns and songs. There the whole culture is an oral one, and it would be interesting to research where people think authority lies, whether in what is known by heart or in the written word because of its rarity.

3. There is another sub-category related to poverty, in inner urban or deeply rural pockets of poverty in otherwise affluent provinces, where the priest would have the book, but the congregation might have only a service leaflet, possibly some years old, and no access to the liturgical riches of a full Prayer Book.

Liturgy Unbound by the Book

4. Another category entirely would include those places where technology and liturgical legislation have enabled liturgy to take a deliberate step of moving beyond the limitations of a book, so that Anglican worship now happens without official printed texts. In England the availability of the text of *Common Worship* – and much more – electronically means there are now many churches which either print their own leaflets, sometimes a new one for each Sunday, sometimes one for each season, or project the texts onto a screen direct from the computer. This has the double advantage of greater flexibility and also means the congregation are looking up, more able to sing and take part, more aware of one another than when their heads are buried in books. The amount of authorized text used will vary from a faithful adherence to the words in the book to the use of very little such material.

5. This is the end of the scale where we should place 'alternative worship', often multi-media and looking fairly unorthodox in Anglican terms, but often within an Anglican building and led by an authorized leader. Some years ago the Liturgical Commission went to a consultation with leaders of some of these groups at Lambeth. The crypt chapel was dark enough for the images projected from underneath the glass-topped communion table to be seen; other images, including part of the text of the 1662 Prayer Book, flashed round the walls. There were no seats apart from some mats on the floor: people were free to move around. The music was piped, loud but easy to get into, and there was no expectation that anyone would sing!

To develop an understanding of where to place all of this in the Anglican spectrum, and to see what it has to say to us, we need to examine the nature of the supposed 'bondage' to the book.

On the green outside Exeter Cathedral you will find a statue of Richard Hooker. I want to quote some words of his on the importance of having a set order for worship, describing liturgy 'bound'!

> 'But of all helps for due performance of this service the greatest is that very set and standing order itself, which framed with common advice, hath both for matter and form [i.e.content and shape] prescribed

whatsoever is herein publicly done. No doubt from God it hath proceeded, and by us it must be acknowledged a work of his singular care and providence, that the Church hath evermore held a prescript form of common prayer.'[19]

'To him which considereth the grievous and scandalous inconveniences whereunto they make themselves daily subject, with whom any blind and secret corner is judged a fit house of common prayer; the manifold confusions which they fall into where every man's private spirit and gift (as they term it) is the only Bishop that ordaineth him to this ministry; the irksome deformities whereby through endless and sense-less effusions of indigested prayers they oftentimes disgrace in most unsufferable manner the worthiest part of Christian duty towards God, who herein are subject to no certain order, but pray both what and how they list: [which shows] why God doth in public prayer so much respect the solemnity of places where, the authority and calling of persons by whom, and the precise appointment even with what words or sentences his name should he called on amongst his people.'[20]

Most people quote Hooker – like Keble - because they feel the need for the approval of this eminent Anglican theologian for some new departure for Anglicanism. I quote him to illustrate how much that view of the Church of England's worship, ministry and buildings was rooted in the 16th century. Though Elizabeth had been on the throne for 38 years when this was published, everyone was aware how volatile and dangerous the political situation was, how hazardous the narrow road between the might and intrigues of Catholic Spain and France and the chaotic but growing force of the puritans who 50 years later would behead the monarch. The need for stability, supported by the conservative traditionalism of the church, was never greater, and Hooker was the man who gave it voice. That view of the church's role lasted for centuries, still exists today, and probably has its spokesmen[21] in this room. And it has nothing to do with churchmanship. The 19th century evangelical Bishop of Liverpool, J.C.Ryle, said:

---

[19] He argues that God framed for 'his priests the very speech wherewith they were charged to bless the people' and that our Lord left the Lord's Prayer 'of purpose to prevent this fancy of extemporal and voluntary prayers'.
[20] R.Hooker, *Ecclesiastical Polity*, Book V. Ch.xxv.4,5
[21] This is a considered use of non-inclusive language.

'it is the mind of God that ministers ... should conduct the worship of Christian congregations, and be responsible for its decent and orderly conduct in approaching God. ... Order is said to be heaven's first law.' [22]

Today our political situation in England and our culture are vastly different from those of Hooker's time, and the part played by the church and its worship in contributing to the stability of society through its life and worship is far more subtle. In many places it is not a matter of restraining the hotheads who want to bring the disorder of the Spirit into church, but of blowing on the dying embers of our congregations in the hope that some semblance of life might prove to be there. I know this is different from place to place, even in England, let alone among the provinces of the church scattered across the world.

But if Hooker's world-view is not to be our starting point for examining the need for liturgical identity, how far back do we go?

Go back to the Bible, and it's not a great deal of help. True, the Old Testament has detailed instructions for sacrificial ceremonial and some pretty lively eye-witness descriptions of worship around the rediscovery of the Book of the Law and its reading by Ezra in Nehemiah 8, with its rubrical instructions, ceremonial actions and responses: there are clearly sacred books which contain what God has caused to be written (nearly but not quite Hooker's view of the BCP), but the culture is very different from the western European culture in which the Church of England came into being. The culture of both people and priests is an oral one, in which an enormous amount of material is known by heart. We have at least one Anglican province with a similar culture, and it would be interesting to hear from them and from others in mainly oral cultures what it is like to find identity with the book-centred culture of other provinces. The New Testament is equally unhelpful. There is little in the way of descriptions of worship apart from the sketchy contents list in Colossians 3 (where the teaching element based on the word of Christ seems to be a mutual exercise) and its echo in Ephesians 5 (not the only place in the New Testament where it seems possible that the thanksgiving was either free or

---

[22] He was also against extempore prayer: 'If all ministers prayed extempore always, as some ministers pray sometimes, I should be against a liturgy. But considering what human nature is, I decidedly think it is better both for minister and people, in the regular, habitual and stated assemblies of the church to have a liturgy.'

raucous enough to be mistaken for drunkenness). As Anglicans with an interest in order we would not of course wish to look for authority to the riotous, divisive, sinful even if sometimes Spirit-filled Church of Corinth, though it is there in 1Corinthians 14, at the end of a description of worship which seems to have everyone expressing themselves in presumably unscripted prophecy, teaching, tongues or revelation, that we find Paul not banning all of that, but expressing the mind of the Church of England: 'let all things be done decently and in order.' And we also owe to the Corinthians and their bad manners at their proto-agape, that description of the Last Supper which we have turned into a liturgical text, though as Paul Bradshaw notes, that did not happen until the fourth century. But if we go hunting for texts to copy into our liturgy, we do not find very much in the NT, a bit in Philippians and Revelation, plus the Lord's Prayer, but perhaps not quite as much as we might have expected from the foundation texts for a church which was ordained to have a wholly written liturgy. But then, the culture was different.

In our hunt for solid textual foundation and rationale we fare almost as badly in the early centuries of the church's life. I guess many of us enjoy liturgical archaeology, and are full of admiration for those who can interpret the fragments of evidence into a cohesive pattern, or use them, as Paul Bradshaw has done in *Eucharistic Origins,* to challenge the received consensus. It is good and valuable – and sometimes provocative – to be able to show ancient precedent for what we do in our worship, and to expose our inherited patterns rigorously to fresh academic insights, and such activity focussing on our common inheritance has made a great contribution to the re-alignment of our liturgical texts so that we experience closer unity with one another and with those in other denominations. But we all know that we do not have all the evidence, nor even a comprehensive picture of what it was like to worship in the third or fourth century. We do not know if there were other structures or shapes apart from the ones we have. We do not know enough about singing or silence or ceremonial to have a definitive picture. We do not know how much was done extempore, (it is in the nature of written text to be recorded and preserved, and in the nature of extempore worship to be unrecorded and ephemeral) though we do have the instruction in the third century *Didascalia Apostolorum* that if a visiting bishop does not want to preside he might at least say the words over the cup.[23] Paul Bradshaw mentions this as part of his argument that the eucharistic prayer was composed, not of a carefully

---

[23] Sebastian Brock and Michael Vasey (eds), *The Liturgical Portions of the Didascalia* (Grove Liturgical Studies No. 29, 1982) p.16

constructed single piece as the *Apostolic Tradition* might lead us to believe, but of a number of units coming together as in the Jewish tradition. And why is there so little evidence of the content of the Word Service until the later fourth century? Could it be either than there was comparatively little written down, or that it was natural for those conserving texts to conserve those which were important for doctrine, for church unity and for catechesis?

So where do we go for our picture of a written liturgical identity if not to the Bible or to the early centuries of the Christian faith? The Reformation came at the right time to create a people of the book, with the widespread application of the invention of printing enabling the imposition by law of a single form of worship across the kingdom. Every parish church, and eventually every worshipper, could have the same text in their hands. The draconian Acts of Uniformity imposing this book and no other form of worship came straight out of that volatile and dangerous political situation I described earlier: it was a matter of national security and identity.[24] This legal position, of being compelled to use the exact words of the book, and nothing but the book, continued formally until the Act of Uniformity Amendment Act 1872.

There was, of course, an interlude in the middle of the 17th century (1645-60) when the Book of Common Prayer was banned and worship was conducted according to the rules of the *Westminster Directory for the Public Worship of God*. This contained instructions for each service, about how to assemble, how to read the scriptures, how to pray (with an example of the latter three pages long). As Ian Breward says in his introduction to the Grove 1980 edition of this text 'It was the first

---

[24] The 1559 Act of Uniformity for instance provided that 'if any manner of parson, vicar, or other whatsoever minister, that ought or should sing or say common prayer mentioned in the said book, or minister the sacraments, ... refuse to use the said common prayers, or to minister the sacraments ... in such order and form as they be set forth in the said book, or shall wilfully or obstinately... use any other rite, ceremony, order, form, ...or shall preach, declare, or speak anything in the derogation or depraving of the said book' then for the first offence, would lose the profit of all his spiritual benefices [for] one whole year next after his conviction; and also [be imprisoned] for six months'; for the second offence imprisonment was for a year, plus deprivation; for the third, deprivation for life and life imprisonment. And it was not just clergy who were affected: 'if any person or persons whatsoever, shall in any interludes, plays, songs, rhymes, or by other open words, declare or speak anything in the derogation, depraving, or despising of the same book, or of anything therein contained, or any part thereof, or shall, by open fact, deed, or by open threatenings, compel or cause, or otherwise procure or maintain, any parson, vicar, or other minister in any cathedral or parish church, or in chapel, or in any other place, to sing or say any common or open prayer, or to minister any sacrament otherwise, or in any other manner and form, than is mentioned in the said book' there was a fine for the first offence and life imprisonment for the second.

attempt after the Reformation to combine order and freedom in a way that demonstrated how reform and liturgy could be profoundly unitive because it was faithfully biblical.' 'How do you secure doctrinal unity and conformity?' was a question which the Church of England had answered, through the Acts of Uniformity, by securing absolute allegiance to texts for worship, the use of which would deliver, over time, conformity of faith to the Reformation ideals, albeit using a traditional, slightly catholic way of doing it. Most of the churches of the Reformation had answered the question by demanding allegiance to a fairly hefty doctrinal statement, leaving the minister far greater freedom in the matter of worship. The Westminster Confession and the *Directory* represent the only time England was tempted in this direction.

The 1872 Act, the result of the Royal Commission on ritual appointed in 1867, allowed for the shortening of Morning and Evening Prayer and provided for an additional service (provided the statutory services were also used) consisting only of material taken directly from the Scriptures or the Prayer Book, but in any form or order the incumbent wished. But whatever the legal position – and this is traced in a chapter on 'The Third Service' in a set of essays by the English Liturgical Commission on *The Renewal of Common Prayer* – there were pressures on the church for alternative worship which regarded the 1872 Act (not replaced until 1965 and only repealed in 1974) as far too timid. There were Sunday School Services, Mission Services and other evangelistic occasions. In 1857 St Jude's Portsea held services for large numbers of people in a former circus building they had bought for the purpose: 'after singing two verses of the National Anthem the more instructive portions of the newspapers are read; a hymn is sung and a prayer offered; the meeting concludes with the doxology.' I was curate at a church in North London which had experienced the 1861 revival – when there were crowds of people at informal evening services, singing and praying in the streets, public confession and testimony in the services, and also – this again showing they were Anglican – the insertion of extempore passages led impromptu by different people, into the General Thanksgiving on Sundays.

Pressure for greater freedom built up in the 20th century, with the defeat of the 1928 Prayer Book (itself the unforeseen result of the Report of the Royal Commission on Ecclesiastical Discipline in 1906), the growth of special services for folk occasions like Mothering Sunday and Harvest, and the growth first of 'Children's Church' and then of Family Services. With the passing of the Prayer Book (Alternative and Other Services) Measure 1965 and the repeal of almost all of the provisions of the Acts of Uniformity in the Worship and Doctrine Measure 1974, the door was wide open to legitimize both the 1928 material and the less formal strands of worship.

In 1986 the Liturgical Commission was grappling with the problem of how to combine common prayer with local freedom, faced with the pressing demands brought about by the growth of the family service culture, often the best attended service yet with both leaders and content unauthorized, and by the needs of inner urban culture expressed in the massive report of the Archbishop of Canterbury's Commission on urban priority areas (UPAs), *Faith in the City* (1985). That report asked for worship to 'emerge out of and reflect local cultures'; to 'be more informal and flexible in its use of urban language ' and 'reflect a universality of form with local variations'. It wanted services which promote a greater involvement of the congregation in worship, and which could be embodied in 'short, functional service booklets or cards. 'The formal liturgies so beloved of the wider church' were to be 'complemented in UPAs by more informal and spontaneous acts of worship and witness.'

A year earlier Douglas Jones, Chairman of the Liturgical Commission, had written, when drafting the Introduction to *Lent, Holy Week, Easter*: 'We are providing a directory from which choices may be made.' That book also included an outline service, consisting only of rubrics, for the Agape with Holy Communion. This was one of the solutions considered by the Commission in looking at combining local freedom with the tradition of common prayer, a solution trailed (with the directory name attached) in the Commission's 1985 report *The Worship of the Church*. In 1986 David Silk and I took from the Commission to the House of Bishops a proposal, which they approved, for the compilation of a 'Directory' – and that was the working title of what became known as *Patterns for Worship* right up to a few months before publication.

This was a very different culture from that of Richard Hooker. How were we to ensure that what we were doing stood within the Anglican tradition? I want to take you back again to Exeter Cathedral, but not to Hooker's statue outside. What do you find inside, today? David Stancliffe introduces his chapter on style in *The Identity of Anglican Worship* with this illustration: 'Now I know why the churches are true', says a four-year-old, watching a televised service from Exeter Cathedral, 'the people in them enjoy singing, and walk about in patterns.' David goes on to develop that peculiarly Anglican mix of spontaneity and order as a way of looking at the patterns of our worship. You will find the same illustration in the original report to Synod of *Patterns for Worship* (1989), in an introductory section on Common Prayer:

> '"common prayer"' exists in the Church of England in the sense of recognizing, as one does when visiting other members of the same family, some common features, some shared experiences, language and patterns or traditions. To accept a variety of forms, dictated by local culture, is part of our Anglican heritage, spelt out by Archbishop Thomas Cranmer in his 1549 Preface: "it often chanceth diversely in diverse countries".
>
> 'What are the marks of Anglican worship that we might expect to find (or have a right to find?) in Family Services or UPA worship. We believe that some of the marks which should be safeguarded for those who wish to stand in any recognizable continuity with historic Anglican tradition are:
> - a recognizable structure for worship
> - an emphasis on reading the word and on using psalms
> - liturgical words repeated by the congregation, some of which, like the creed, would be known by heart
> - using a collect, the Lord's Prayer, and some responsive forms in prayer
> - a recognition of the centrality of the Eucharist
> - a concern for form, dignity, and economy of words: as the four-year-old said about Church of England services, "the people in them enjoy singing, and walk about in patterns."'

I quoted this when in 1993 I introduced *A Service of the Word*, the service at the heart of *Patterns*, to the General Synod, and addressed the issues about common prayer which inevitably arise when you authorize a service with almost no text apart from a set of rubrical instructions. I noted what 'was happening in the international sphere, with province after province moving away from the old "glue" of 1662 which some thought held the Communion together, and producing new Prayer Books which were still very evidently part of the same family of Anglican common prayer. And it is worth noting that some of those books contain outline services similar to that before you today - only some have gone further and produced a similar outline for the eucharist too. There is either an international conspiracy of liturgists or a very strong family bond that makes our worship "common": perhaps both?' And, with a slightly tongue-in-cheek glance at the 17th century *Directory* – and to allay some people's fears - I noted that 'We also put in an appendix to

Patterns for Worship the doctrinal summary from the *Code of Practice for the Ecumenical Canons*, which summarizes the provisions of Canon A5 and the 1974 Measure about conformity to the doctrine of the Church of England, and indicates where to look for that doctrine - in the Holy Scriptures, the Fathers and Councils of the church, the Thirty-nine Articles, the Book of Common Prayer and the Ordinal and such forms of service, canons and regulations as have received the final approval of General Synod'. I also quoted from *The Renewal of Common Prayer* published that year 'Is it inevitable that creativity at congregational level will mean that English Anglicans can no longer feel at home in different parish churches? Must the sensitive adaptation of worship to local culture lead to the formation of personal patterns of devotion that are more parochial than national or catholic? Are liturgical anarchy and the fragmentation of personal spirituality an inevitable result of increasing deregulation of public worship? The answer, in the mind of the Commission, is to give attention to the evolving core of the Church's common prayer.' That core we saw as containing both clear and familiar structures, and some texts which everyone knew.

Patterns for Worship was for use published in 1995; its white, red, blue and yellow Mondrian-like cover captured the patterns idea well and proclaimed that it was unlike any other official worship book. It combined both authorized and commended liturgical texts, a large amount of educational material, and sixteen Sample Services with illustrations by the cartoonist Taffy. It immediately sold out, went into a number of reprints, and sold over ten thousand copies in under two years. It was also remarkable in that each text had a distinctive number, the beginning of the electronic database which was at the heart of the Church's service compilation programme, *Visual Liturgy*, which came out eighteen months later. This contained *Patterns* as well as the whole of the ASB, material from two Bibles for three lectionaries and nearly three thousand hymns and songs. The effect of combining 'A Service of the Word' with electronic publishing was that what had begun as an exercise in inculturation, making local choice and creativity in worship more possible (and it did that), now made it possible for any local church to access, through extra modules and through the internet, large amounts of adventurous and often unauthorized material. Does this matter?

Go back to the Commission's view of the 'evolving core' of Anglican worship – structures and shared texts. We were clear about the importance of structure or shape: 'People are more likely to be able to cope with alternative prayers, eucharistic prayers, canticles, intercessions, if they know exactly where they are likely to come. There is an issue of liturgical formation here: once there is a rhythm, there is a greater chance of people expecting the liturgy to make sense.'[25] If you have clear and familiar shape, it also matters a lot less whether the text is written down: you know what is happening from the point you are at in the service, without the need to read the text. The 1662 Prayer Book has no section headings, and the structure is not all that clear to newcomers to the service, so it is as well to have a text. One of the major contributions of the IALC has been to produce agreed suggestions for the structures of eucharist, initiation and the ordinal.

With the computer programme *Visual Liturgy*, though it is possible to access the database in a fairly random way and discover that there are 300 different blessings or 200 confessions, the normal mode of access is in a very ordered, calendrically-based approach, via a template designed to display the basic structure of the service: your first stop in creating a service is the calendar, your second is a template with the three or four main headings of the service. It is deliberately designed (and I should know because I designed it!) to promote a structural approach to the liturgy, a structural approach which is echoed in detail in the educational material in *New Patterns for Worship* (2002) on how to put a service together.

That does not sound like an abandonment of Anglican worship, but an aid to reinforcing those very elements in common prayer which the Commission outlined in 1989 – clear structures, using some texts known by heart like the Lord's Prayer, emphasizing both the word of God and the centrality of the eucharist, and a concern for form, dignity and economy of words.

It must be fairly clear by now that I think that this issue should lead us to look for the glue which holds us together in the areas of shape, minimal content, and less tangible things than rigid adherence to liturgical texts or confessions of faith. It is more difficult, because there is no absolute standard by which we can judge that someone has departed from the norm, and because it demands a lot of those responsible for teaching and liturgical formation, but it is a more organic approach which is leading to that kind of growth and creativity within the churches of our family for which we all long.

---

[25] Kenneth Stevenson in *The Renewal of Common Prayer*, p.12

4 'Remembering the Future': Reflections on Liturgy and Ecclesiology

Louis Weil

In the eucharistic prayer of St. John Chrysostom, in a phrase which proclaims the great events of salvation history in the life of Jesus Christ, the anamnesis refers to an event which has not yet taken place: 'Remembering ... the second and glorious coming again.'[26] I have always found this a remarkable phrase in the context of an anamnesis because our natural expectation in an act of remembering is in reference to events in the past. For years I have called the attention of my students to this phrase, noting how unusual it is in this context, and interpreting its presence in this eucharistic prayer as a kind of completion of the circle of events in salvation history, culminating in the consummation at the end of time.

More recently, I have found in this remembrance of the future a related insight: our need to reflect on the imperative of an eschatological perspective in the liturgy. British Roman Catholic theologian Paul McPartlan has written that 'The Church's centre of gravity lies in the future, not in the past.'[27] This insight, it seems to me, offers a radical corrective to our tendency to see Christian liturgical actions as grounded in past events, and, more specifically with regard to the eucharist, in reference to the final meal which Jesus held with his disciples. Over the centuries, extraordinary effort has gone into attempts to explain how the Church's celebration of the eucharist, many centuries removed from that final meal, is linked to the events of those last days in the life of Jesus: the meal, the death and the resurrection. Would placing those events into the context of the Church's future fulfilment offer us new insights into their meaning?

---

[26] R.C.D. Jasper and G.J. Cuming, *Prayers of the Eucharist: Early and Reformed* (Pueblo Publishing Co., New York, 1987) p. 133.
[27] Paul McPartlan, *The Eucharist Makes the Church* (T & T Clark, Edinburgh, 1993) p. 187.

Following McPartlan's statement that the eucharist receives its fulfilment, what he calls its 'centre of gravity', from the future, points us toward the promise of the future gathering of all the people of God around Christ at the end of time. This is the promise of the heavenly banquet found in both the Old and New Testaments: this is the eschatological assembly of which each celebration of the eucharist is a foretaste (cf. e.g. Is.25.6 Heb.12.22-24). I want to explore the issues which cluster around this claim.

Paul Bradshaw originally asked me to present a paper at the IALC meeting in Prague on 'Liturgy and Ecclesiology'. I recognized immediately that the relevant questions are vast in extent, and that I would be obliged to focus on some particular aspect of the subject. My musings led me first to the Nicene Creed in which, at celebrations of the eucharist, we profess our faith in 'one holy catholic and apostolic Church', adjectives which spell out what are commonly called the four marks of the Church.

I decided to focus on the first of these, the 'one', that is, the unity of the Church. My reason for this is obvious. Virtually all the documentation regarding the current crisis in the Anglican Communion revolves around the issue of unity: can the presumed unity indicated by the phrase 'the Anglican Communion' be maintained? Is schism inevitable? Is the unity of the Anglican Communion about to be shattered? Under such circumstances we are all required to reflect deeply on questions which are larger in scope than our own crisis, namely, what is the nature of the unity of the Church which we profess in the Creed? How is that unity embodied in the sharing of the eucharistic gifts? And what would be the impact of placing these questions within an eschatological context?

Before turning to these questions, as a brief preliminary, I want to make a general observation about how 'the Church' has been understood in Anglicanism. We may begin with a citation from Richard Hooker. He writes: 'By the Church ... we understand no other than only the visible

Church.'[28] He then notes that this one Catholic Church is 'divided into a number of distinct Societies.' Hooker's word 'Societies' would seem to equate with what we would call 'denominations', or 'communions', or, in a derivative sense, 'churches'. We as Anglicans might say that there is only one Church, of which we are 'an ecclesial communion'.

I have begun with this quotation from Hooker because I think that it is important to take as a reference point his emphasis that this Church is visible, that is, as a society whose life unfolds in human history, and that this one visible Church is in fact divided into 'a number of distinct Societies'. Hooker thus affirms that the essential unity of the one Church is not nullified by the fact of division. He is affirming a unity which is so fundamental to the Church's nature that it transcends the reality of division. We might want to note that his phrase 'distinct Societies' implies nothing more than benign divisions, perhaps merely geographical in nature, although even in his own time those divisions, as between the English Church and the Church of Rome, were by no means benign. In our time, many such divisions are often adversarial in character.

The unity of this visible Church of which Hooker speaks is not merely a unity of organization, such as can be found in many human societies which are united, for example, in some social service and might have no religious identity at all. This would be a purely human unity of people united in some shared activity and maintained by human effort. This certainly does not apply to the Church's unity since the opposite has been all too evident: the human contribution to the Church's life can often be identified with the creation of divisions. As E.L. Mascall has written:

> '... the Church is made one by a unifying principle which, while it works in men and binds them both to one another and to Christ their Lord, has supervened and still supervenes upon them from outside themselves and unites them in a way beyond anything that their own activity could achieve.'[29]

---

[28] *The Laws of Ecclesiastical Polity*, Book III, Ch. 1, Par. 14 (in J.Keble (ed) *Works*, Vol 1, p.351)
[29] E.L. Mascall, *Corpus Christi* (Longmans, Green and Co., London, 1953) p. 4.

Given the evident divisions in the visible Church, what then is this unity which we profess as an article of faith in the Nicene Creed? To what is the Creed referring when it professes that the Church is 'one'? It would, of course, be absurd to claim that this is a numerical unity. Last month an article appeared in *Christianity Today* which noted that, statistically, there are some 37,000 'associations' on our planet which identify themselves as 'the Church of Jesus Christ'. The author adds that, even if one eliminates the splinter groups, there would still be some 25,000 distinct ecclesial (in some sense of that word) societies.[30] One would not have to know a great deal about Church history to be aware that adversarial divisions are not new for the Church. Conflict and schism can be found in every era of the Church's history, as the Dominican ecumenist J.-M. R. Tillard has remarked:

> '..... the history of the Church can be viewed ... as marked by splits ... which always leave their mark. We have examples dating from the frictions of the Greeks and the Hebrews, the conflicts between disciples of James and Christians who had come over from paganism, and the tensions between the Johannine communities and others. Communion does not shine forth in all its splendor except on too few occasions, even if the obstacles that are perceived in the New Testament do not necessarily indicate a break or separation. Rarely has communion been realized in its perfection on the universal plane.'[31]

If unity is a 'mark' of the Church's essential nature, a mark which has, as Tillard says, rarely been perfectly realized, then does an eschatological perspective - the idea of a realization which lies in the future where, quoting McPartlan, the Church's 'centre of gravity is found' - does this orientate our understanding of the unity of the Church in a more realistic yet theologically substantial way? And how would we understand the role of the liturgy within the context of this orientation? What do our liturgical rites, and particularly the sacraments of baptism and eucharist, say to us about the unity of the Church?

In this essay, I act on the presumption that these two sacraments are the primary liturgical embodiment of the prayer of Christ for his disciples, and thus for the Church, 'ut unum sint' ('that they may all be one', John 17.11). With regard to baptism, my focus will be upon a baptismal

---

[30] Timothy George, 'Is Christ Divided?' in *Christianity Today* (July 2005) pp. 31–33.
[31] J.-M. R. Tillard, *Church of Churches: The Ecclesiology of Communion* (Liturgical Press, Collegeville, MN, 1992) p. 33.

ecclesiology, that is, a defining of the unity of the Church as grounded in the identity shared by all baptized Christians: the Church as the body of Christ. What does this unity, effected by baptism, mean when we look honestly at the evident divisions among Christians?

With regard to the eucharist, my focus is upon the role of the Holy Spirit in every proclamation of the Great Prayer of Thanksgiving, which is the heart of the eucharistic action. I see this work of the Spirit as an essential expression of the unity which baptism effects. In the eucharistic prayer, the Spirit's activity has been generally understood as ordered toward both the unity of Christians through the Spirit's agency in the consecration of the gifts, and the people's sharing of those gifts, the sacramental body and blood of the Lord, as the outward sign of their common faith.[32] How are we to interpret the work of the Holy Spirit as the agent of Christian unity when Christian churches celebrate a eucharist at which Christians of other traditions are not welcome as communicants?

So we need to consider two closely related sacramental acts: the unity manifested through baptism and the unity manifested through eucharistic communion. What would be the effect of placing these acts within an eschatological perspective? How might we come to see unity not as an idealized norm from the past which has in fact been shattered throughout much of the Church's history? Might we see this unity rather as a promise of the future fulfilment toward which baptism and eucharist orient the Church?

Baptismal Ecclesiology and Disunity

In the ecumenical dialogues between the various Christian traditions, agreements on baptism and eucharist have been generally easy to achieve. The truly divisive issues have tended to cluster around the diverse models of ordained leadership in the various traditions and the closely related issue of ministerial authority.[33] From what was said earlier, it seems that the significant agreement on the theologies of baptism and eucharist which has been achieved in the various ecumenical documents might offer a basis upon which a greater degree of unity and intercommunion might be realized.

---

[32] Cf. my article, 'Holy Spirit: Source of Unity in the Liturgy' in R.B.Slocum (ed), *Engaging the Spirit* (Church Publishing, New York, 2001) pp. 39-45. Thus we may appropriately speak not only of the real presence of Christ in the eucharist, but also of the real presence of the Holy Spirit.

[33] Cf. my 'Baptismal Ecclesiology: Uncovering a Paradigm' in Ronald L.Dowling and David R.Holeton (eds), *Equipping the Saints: Ordination in Anglicanism Today* (The Columba Press, Dublin, 2006) pp. 18-34.

Such an advance is inhibited, of course, by the familiar presupposition that Christians of different traditions should not share communion until all disputed questions have been reconciled. In this approach, intercommunion is possible only when disagreements regarding faith and practice have been resolved. In this view, communion becomes the sign of a unity already achieved. This view was stated in the Report of the Fourth World Conference on Faith and Order in these words:

> 'Some Christians believe that eucharistic communion, being an expression of the acceptance of the whole Christ, implies full unity in the wholeness of his truth; that there cannot be any "intercommunion" between otherwise separated Christians; that communion in the sacraments therefore implies a pattern of doctrine and ministry which is indivisible; and that "intercommunion" cannot presume upon the union in faith that we still seek.'[34]

Given the reality of institutional divisions which have been characteristic of the Church for at least a millennium (if we think first of the Great Schism between East and West in 1054), but which can be found on a lesser scale throughout the Church's history, it was inevitable that division would affect the sharing of eucharistic communion. In that context, inter-communion was inconceivable without the complete resolution of all the issues which divided the respective ecclesial bodies. The unity created by the one baptism was undermined by the impact of a schismatic spirit, fostered by a context of power issues, and thus unity in eucharistic communion ceased.

Within the context of a baptismal ecclesiology, however, differences in doctrine, for example, would not be seen as the defining characteristics separating one ecclesial tradition from another, but rather as differences within the one body made up of all the baptized. In other words, a baptismal ecclesiology rests upon the foundation we find in Paul's words: 'There is one body, and one Spirit ... one Lord, one faith, one baptism, one God and Father of us all, who is above all and through all and in all.' (Eph.4.4-6). The vision presented here is one which would embrace differences among Christians as inviting dialogue and the sharing

---

[34] P.C. Rodger and L. Vischer (eds), *Report of the Fourth World Conference on Faith and Order, Montreal 1963* (Faith and Order Paper No. 42, World Council of Churches, London) p. 78, para. 139.

of faith experience, and as a summons to a higher commitment of unity in Christ, a unity which is not menaced by diversity. This may seem to be naively optimistic, but it does take seriously the unity which Baptism effects. This is the view that was put forth at the same Conference on Faith and Order in these words:

> 'Some Christians believe that the degree of ecclesial communion which we have in the body of Christ, through baptism and through our fundamental faith, although we are still divided on some points, urges us to celebrate Holy Communion together and to promote intercommunion between the churches. It is Christ, present in the Eucharist, who invites all Christians to his table: this direct invitation of Christ cannot be thwarted by ecclesiastical discipline. In the communion at the same holy table, divided Christians are committed in a decisive way to make manifest their total, visible and organic unity.'[35]

This alternative theological approach to the relation of intercommunion to Christian unity, sees the eucharist as an effective or causative sign of unity, that is, that the eucharist embodies the grace to effect the unity which it signifies.[36] On the whole, this second approach has received rather modest attention. It is, however, a strong expression of the implications of a baptismal ecclesiology. The assumption on which it rests is that baptism creates the unity of the one Church, and that although human sin may scar that unity, it cannot annihilate it.

Intercommunion grounded in the one baptism is orientated toward the future. It sees the divisions in the Church as real but not ultimate, and is thus orientated toward the hoped-for fulfilment when all of God's people will be gathered in unity around their Lord at the eschaton. This second approach is thus clearly eschatological in its orientation.

The recovery of a baptismal ecclesiology will necessarily require a creative engagement with the clerical ecclesiology which has dominated the

---

[35] *Op.cit.,* para. 138.
[36] I am indebted to the Dominican liturgical scholar, Irenèe Dalmais, who first called my attention to this other theological foundation for intercommunion.

Church's self-understanding for well over a millennium. Although there are authentic values in the heritage of the ecclesiology which has shaped all of us, whether laity or clergy, what is required is a transformation of the Church's self-understanding in ways which incorporate the vision of a baptismal ecclesiology.

The British theologian, Paul Avis, has brought this helpful insight to these questions. He writes:
> 'We need to work for greater mutual understanding in the context of total mutual acceptance on the basis of our baptism into Christ and the fundamental Trinitarian baptismal faith of the Church. This can be done, I believe, without sacrificing or compromising what is distinctive and precious in our own tradition. This is the key to finding a new paradigm for Anglicanism, and indeed for ecumenical Christianity.'[37]

What Avis calls 'a new paradigm' is an ecclesiology which begins from the essential unity of the one Church of Jesus Christ into which we have been baptized. But the understanding which flows out of mutual acceptance is more easily affirmed than achieved. Again, the one Church is the Church in human history, a community of faith in which human fallibility is a constant factor in the all-too-human tendency toward ideological separation.

Eschatology and Unity

Recently, there has been extensive discussion among the primates of the Anglican Communion and also in the wider Church about consequences for communion of the decisions of the American Church to ordain to the episcopate a partnered gay man, and the decision in the Church of Canada (in the diocese of New Westminster) to authorize the blessing of same-sex unions.[38] Although these are the presenting issues of the current crisis, they are clearly related to the larger questions raised at the beginning of this paper: what is the nature of the unity of the Church which we profess in the Nicene Creed? How is that unity embodied in the sharing of the eucharistic gifts? And what would be the impact of placing these questions within an eschatological context?

---

[37] Paul Avis, *Anglicanism and the Christian Church* (T & T Clark, London, 2002) p. 346.
[38] On this issue, cf. my article, 'Rome and Canterbury—Steps Toward Reconciliation Through the Sharing of Gifts' in *Semi-annual Bulletin* (Centro Pro Unione, Rome, No. 67, Spring 2005) pp. 16-20.

First I must speak about the issue of unity at a universal level. Orthodox theologian John Zizioulas has written that 'Ecclesial unity on a universal level is essential for the Eucharist'.[39] He urges that it is the work of the councils of the Church to re-receive the truths of the faith for their own times. This re-reception takes place ultimately in the eucharistic celebrations of the local churches. Zizioulas describes this process as follows:

> '... each local church receives the gospel and re-receives it constantly through the ministry of the *episcope* acting in communion with the faithful and with the other local churches in conciliar decisions through a universal primacy.'[40]

With regard to this 'universal primacy', Zizioulas comments that 'one should not hesitate to seek such a ministry in the Bishop of Rome.'[41] Remembering that Zizioulas is an Orthodox, we need to see the sense in which that universal primacy would, for him, be exercised by the Bishop of Rome. In Orthodox ecclesiology, each local church is the Catholic Church; each bishop is the successor of Peter. One might say that each local church is presided over by Peter and the apostles. In this model, the pope would not be Peter and other bishops the apostolic college, but rather the pope would be Peter in the Church of Rome, and, by virtue of that, *primus inter pares* in his relation to other bishops, each of whom is understood to represent Peter in each of the various local churches, with the college of presbyters representing the apostolic college.

For Anglicans, it is useful in this context to consider the revisioned role of the Bishop of Rome proposed in the ARCIC Statement *The Gift of Authority* which was published in 1998.[42] In the discussion of primacy, the document presents a restrained interpretation of how papal primacy has functioned in the Church historically. The document refers appropriately to the role played by St. Leo the Great in his contribution

---

[39] J.Zizioulas 'The ecclesiological presuppositions of the holy Eucharist' in *Nicolaus* 10 (1982) p. 347.
[40] J.Zizioulas 'The Theological Problem of "Reception"' in *One in Christ* 21 (1985) p. 192.
[41] *Ibid.*
[42] *The Gift of Authority. Authority in the Church III.* An Agreed Statement by the Second Anglican–Roman Catholic International Commission (Church Publishing, New York) 1999.

to the Council of Chalcedon as being of benefit to the whole Church, and also, with reference to SS. Gregory the Great and Augustine of Canterbury, how the papacy has served to the benefit of local churches. In reference to the defining of the faith of the Church, ARCIC-2's casting of the role of the papacy, certainly as it has come to be conceived, can only be termed 'naïve'. Definitions of the faith of the Church are, the document says,

> 'pronounced within the college of those who exercise episcope and not outside that college. Such authoritative teaching is a particular exercise of the calling and responsibility of the body of bishops to teach and affirm the faith. When the faith is articulated in this way, the Bishop of Rome proclaims the faith of the local churches. It is thus the wholly reliable teaching of the whole Church that is operative in the judgement of the universal primate.'[43]

My problem here is that this claim overlooks the impact of the pontificate of Pius IX, who proclaimed the Dogma of the Immaculate Conception by his own authority alone in 1854. That model of papal authority was then sealed with the Dogma of Infallibility promulgated at Vatican 1 in 1870. In this context, the universal primacy is exercised by the Bishop of Rome without any required consultation with his fellow bishops within the Roman Communion, not to mention even the hint of such consultation with the bishops of the churches which are not in communion with Rome.

My second problem with the quotation from *The Gift of Authority*, which I shall note here only in passing but which is of enormous significance, is its identification of 'authoritative teaching' in the Church as the 'responsibility of the body of bishops ... and not outside that college', without reference to the *consensus fidelium* and the question of the reception of doctrine by the whole Church.

---

[43] *The Gift of Authority*, paras. 46-47.

In spite of ARCIC and Rome's other dialogues with its ecumenical partners, this revisioned model of papal authority which *The Gift of Authority* presents is by no means in evidence. In an address presented at the Secretariat of Unity in Rome in 1967, Pope Paul VI acknowledged that 'The papacy ... is without doubt the most grave obstacle on the ecumenical road.'[44] This would seem to call for nothing less than a revolution in the official understanding of the papal office in the Roman Church, a revolution which the dominant ultramontane voices are not prepared to accept. If anything, the monarchical model of the papacy, so clearly triumphant in the 19th-century pontificate of Pope Pius IX and in the decrees of Vatican I, has continued to strengthen in the century and a half since that time. For Rome, the pope in his person embodies the unity of the visible Church. On this point, it is sobering to remember the words of Pius IX to Cardinal Filippo Maria Guidi after the cardinal had made a proposal at the Council which was conciliatory to the opponents of the definition. Guidi said that the definition of papal infallibility would be contrary to tradition, to which Pius IX replied, 'Tradition? I am tradition. I am the Church.'[45]

In the light of this reality, the affirmation of Zizioulas that 'Ecclesial unity on a universal level is essential for the Eucharist' must be seen as an idealized ecclesiology or, as I would suggest, as expressive of an eschatological ecclesiology. The English Methodist theologian Geoffrey Wainwright offers a schema of the related issues regarding the eucharist, Christian unity and eschatology. He writes that 'the eschatological nature of the eucharist impels divided Christians towards the practice of intercommunion'.[46] When Christians are divided, Wainwright suggests, there can be no satisfactory doctrinal formulation of the relation between the Church and the sacraments.

---

[44] *Documentation catholique* 64 (1967) 870; *AAS* 59,7 (1967) 498. See my 'The Papacy: An Obstacle or a Sign for Christian Unity?' in *International Journal for the Study of the Christian Church* (Vol. 4, No. 1), March 2004, pp. 6–20. See also, Colin Buchanan, *Is Papal Authority a Gift for Us?* (Grove Books, Cambridge, 2003).
[45] Hans Küng, *Infallible?* (Collins, London, 1971) pp. 106–107; August Bernhard Hasler, *How the Pope Became Infallible* (Doubleday, New York, 1981) pp. 89-92; *passim.*
[46] G.Wainwright, *Eucharist and Eschatology* (Oxford University Press, New York, 1981) p. 137.

The fundamental anomaly is our divisions, yet that is the real world in which we live. Because of this profound anomaly, all celebrations of the eucharist in all of the various Christian traditions are in some sense impaired, because they point to an ecclesial unity which is not a lived reality for the Church in our world. For Roman Catholicism the answer to this dilemma is that only celebrations of the eucharist at which a priest in communion with the Holy See presides can fulfil that signification because only the Roman Church gives validation to such sacramental acts. Edward Schillebeeckx, in *Christ the Sacrament of the Encounter with God*, long before the ecumenical achievements of recent decades, dared as a Roman Catholic theologian to question this assertion and to propose that celebrations of the eucharist by Christians who are not in communion with Rome are nevertheless ordered toward the same end as the Roman Catholic Mass.[47]

In the light of this, it would perhaps be appropriate for Anglicans around the world not to be too myopic about the current threat to communion forced upon us by fundamentalist, neo-puritan voices who are seeking separation from the 'tainted' American and Canadian churches. In saying this, I am by no means suggesting that further schism is desirable. Yet we are more aware today than in past generations how often what we might call 'conflicting truths' are grounded in widely divergent cultural contexts. Bridging these divides is a more arduous task than our religious structures have been willing to acknowledge. The threat of schism is all too real when widely differing cultural 'languages' can find no meeting point. We are then left with the problem of differing understandings of truth and with very different approaches as to how the Scriptures are to be interpreted.

---

[47] E. Schillebeeckx, *Christ the Sacrament of the Encounter with God* (Sheed and Ward, New York, 1964) pp.184-195.

As we saw earlier, there is a well-established tradition in Christianity that unity in faith (and this would include, it seems, unity in regard to the interpretation of Scripture) must be a prerequisite for the sharing of communion. Where this view is in force, simple honesty must oblige us to admit that significant barriers to the sharing of communion already exist. Schism has taken place in the past, and, sadly, may occur again in the days ahead. Yet our unity in the one baptism establishes our unity in the one Church in spite of our sinful divisions.

Wainwright is again helpful in this regard. He writes of the contrast between 'the Lord's supper and the church's supper':

> 'In a state of affairs marred by human sin (and Christian disunity is such a state), we may be obliged to choose between the order Christ-church-sacraments and Christ-sacraments-church. In that case the choice must fall in favour of the second... The need to choose, and then this positive choice, are forced upon us by the fact that human sin may cause a degree of separation between the church and its Lord (and result in a division among Christians and in faulty performance of the sacraments which the Lord has given His church to perform as signs by which to enjoy and proclaim the kingdom of God) but that the sacraments remain the Lord's entirely, and may be used by Him, even when (at the purely human level) defectively performed, as the vehicles of His presence to bring His church to a more obedient acknowledgement ... of the kingdom of God. In the light of this eschatological purpose, no obstacle of ecclesiastical discipline dependent on a sinful state of Christian disunity must be allowed to block the Lord's invitation to all penitents among His sinning people to gather round His table wherever it is set up and to receive His forgiveness for sins that have led to disunity and be filled through His transforming presence with the love that unites.' [48]

In the face of Christian disunity, and the possibility of further division, our divided Christian traditions are obliged to acknowledge the provisional character of all celebrations of the eucharist. The eschatological nature of the eucharist suggested here always points us to

---

[48] *Loc.cit.*

future fulfilment. Our celebration of the eucharist here on earth is a foretaste of that heavenly banquet which Scripture holds out to us as a promise of the future when all of God's people will be gathered in unity around Christ in the kingdom of God.

We may appropriately invoke here a teaching which we find in the early Fathers, both East and West. Irenaeus is thought to have been the first to have said, 'God made himself man, that man might become God', or, as we might say today, 'God became a human person so that we might be united with God.'[49] We find this teaching also in Athanasius, Gregory Nazianzus, and Gregory of Nyssa, and repeated by theologians, particularly of the Eastern churches, in every century since. Vladimir Lossky writes that we find 'in this striking sentence the very essence of Christianity: an ineffable descent of God to the ultimate limit of our fallen human condition, even unto death - a descent of God which opens to men a path of ascent, the unlimited vistas of the union of created beings with the Divinity.'[50]

Lossky is referring to what theologians call entheosis or deification. Donald Allchin has shown the place which this theology has in the Anglican tradition, beginning with Richard Hooker, and including Lancelot Andrewes, Charles Wesley, and E.B. Pusey. Allchin contends that

> '... the doctrine of our deification, our becoming partakers of the divine nature by God's grace, is inseparably and necessarily bound up with the other two doctrines which stand at the heart of classical Christian faith and life, the doctrine of God as Trinity, and the doctrine of the incarnation of God the Word. All three doctrines belong together, and it may be our neglect of the one which has made us uncertain about the others. ... God who is utterly beyond his creation yet comes to be present at the heart of his creation comes to identify himself with his creation in order to lift it up into union with himself. This union, established once for all in Christ, is constantly renewed in varying ways in the coming of the Spirit.'[51]

---

[49] *Adversus haereses* V, preface.
[50] Vladimir Lossky, *In the Image and Likeness of God* (London, 1975) p. 97.
[51] A.M. Allchin, *Participation in God* (Morehouse-Barlow, Wilton, CN, 1988) p.5.

'Remembering the Future': Reflections on Liturgy and Ecclesiology

Deification is thus the eschatological hope of Christians, the fulfilment of God's acts in creation, the incarnation, and in the sending of the Holy Spirit. Orthodox theologian Panayiotis Nellas identifies the end of this eschatological hope as 'the transformation of the universe'.[52] The deification of our humanity is thus integral to God's cosmic purpose for the whole of creation. We find here a confirmation of Paul McPartlan's claim that 'The Church's centre of gravity lies in the future, not in the past'.[53]

But what does this have to do with our subject? A great deal, I think. This 'union of created beings with the Divinity', of which Lossky speaks, this deification, has been understood as the fulfilment of the promise that God has 'given us his very great and precious promises so that through them you may participate in the divine nature' (2 Pet.1.4). It is through this participation in the divine nature that Christians are united. It is this participation that transcends the inevitable divisions and conflicts of fallible human beings. When the Nicene Creed proclaims that the Church is one, it is of this unity that the Creed is speaking. And it is through baptism that we are incorporated into that unity. It is in baptism that each one of us is set upon the path which can only find its fulfilment in the eschaton, at the end of time when God will be all in all. As we pursue that path, it is the eucharist that embodies the promise initiated in baptism by sustaining us with the grace of the Holy Spirit who orientates us again and again toward our goal, unity with and in God.

In this we see the significance of the anamnesis in the eucharistic prayer of St. John Chrysostom to which I referred at the start: we remember 'the second and glorious coming again'. We remember the future in which the unity to which the eucharist points will be accomplished. It is that eschatological unity which is the mark of the Church and the goal toward which the life of the Church is ordered.

---

[52] P. Nellas, *Deification in Christ. The Nature of the Human Person* (St. Vladimir's Seminary Press, Crestwood, New York, 1987) pp.157-159.
[53] P. McPartlan, *The Eucharist Makes the Church*, p. 187.

Appendix: Liturgy and Anglican Identity

A Discussion Document by the International Anglican Liturgical Consultation, Prague, August 2005.

We believe that Anglican identity is expressed and formed through our liturgical tradition of corporate worship and private prayer, holding in balance both word and sacramental celebration. Specifically, our tradition is located within the broad and largely western stream of Christian liturgical development but has been influenced by eastern liturgical forms as well.

The importance of the eucharist and the pattern of daily prayer were refocused through the lens of the Reformation, making both accessible to the people of God through simplification of structure and text and the use of vernacular language. Through the exchanges and relationships between the Provinces of the Anglican Communion the legacy of these historic principles continues to inform the on-going revision of our rites and their enactment in the offering to God of our worship. Each Province of the Anglican Communion has its own story to tell, and although within the Communion we are bound together by a common history, what really unites us, as with all Christians, is our one-ness in Christ through baptism and the eucharist. Our unity in baptism and at the table of the Lord is both a gift and a task. We celebrate our unity in Christ and seek to realize that unity through the diversity of backgrounds and cultures within the compass of the world-wide Anglican Communion.

Recognizing the role of the bishop as a symbol of unity and the partnership of ordained and lay, clergy and people, we value a leadership which is competent and liturgically formed and seeks to engage local culture, language and custom within a vision of what holds us together as part of the one, holy, catholic and apostolic church. We value a view of leadership which sees the leader of worship as a servant who enables people to worship in a way that has integrity within their own experience, customs, and gifts.

We value and celebrate the ways in which we have been formed by and within our customs to attend to the grace of God, invoked and celebrated in our public prayer, and active in our lives and in the world around us.

Ethos/Elements: we value

Worship that includes and honours the proclamation of the word and celebrates the sacraments of baptism and eucharist.

An inherited tradition that holds together both catholic and reformed.

The fact that we have texts which are authorized.

Freedom for varieties of expression.

The aesthetic potential of environment, music, art, and movement, offered as appropriate to the culture.

The symbiotic relationship between corporate worship and individual piety.

Worship in an ordered liturgical space.

The liturgical ministry of bishops, priests and deacons.

We value the following characteristics in our rites.

Shape (see the 1991 Toronto Statement of the IALC, *Walk in Newness of Life*, for its treatment of the structure of the baptismal rite, and the 1995 Dublin Statement of the IALC, for descriptive notes on the structure of the eucharistic rite).

Extensive reading of scripture.

Lectionary.

Rhythms of year, week, day.

Regular celebration of Holy Communion.

Baptism in public worship.

Prayers which include thanksgiving, (general) confession, intercessions.

Extensive intercessions - focusing on the world, those in authority and the world church before local concerns, and including concern for those whose lives are shadowed by poverty, sickness, rejection, war, and natural disaster.

Use of the Lord's Prayer.

Use of responsive texts.

Knowing words, music, and actions by heart.

Common prayers.

Corporate and participatory worship.

Use of Creeds in worship.

The openness and accessibility of our worship.

V Some Anglican emphases, trends and aspirations.

In worship, we are drawn into a living relationship with the Triune God in patterns of prayer that are in themselves Trinitarian in form and content, and invite us to enter more deeply into God's life and love as those who are called to be 'partakers of the divine nature' (2 Peter 1.4). In our coming before God in adoration and thanksgiving, penitence and prayer, we recognize that liturgical celebration is both our corporate action, our work, words and ritual gestures, and also an occasion when God, through the Holy Spirit, is active and at work making and re-making our lives.

Our worship is rooted in God's work of creation, incarnation and redemption and so needs to be embodied and enacted in ways that engage all the senses. Thus we honour the goodness of creation, pray for its healing, and come to delight in splendour as we celebrate both the beauty of holiness and the holiness of beauty.

We recognize that God's creation is often disfigured by sin, by human greed and violence, and we seek that healing grace which flows from the cross of Christ. As we commemorate Christ's saving death and transfiguring resurrection in the celebration of the eucharist we are again made one in him and strengthened to witness to his reconciling love in our broken world.

Appendix

We invoke the Holy Spirit, seeking to be open to God's future, and to orient ourselves to the fulfilling of God's purposes. Recognizing this essential eschatological dimension of Christian worship, we seek to attend to the various relationships that transcend both space and time: our sharing in the Communion of Saints, with our Anglican brothers and sisters around the globe, and with the whole oikoumene. Through our conversations and engagement with each other in the work of Christ we seek to realize more fully the unity that God has given us and to which Christ calls us.

We believe that our worship conveys and carries the historic faith of the Church, and recognize that as we are blessed with reason, memory and skill we are called to use our gifts in crafting liturgy that honours our received and living faith in this time and context.

We believe that the rhythm of worship, our gathering and our being 'sent out', mirrors the mission of God, of God's engagement with the world and the claims of God's Kingdom of justice, righteousness and peace. We therefore commend again the inseparable relation between worship and mission. (cf. the 'marks of mission' preamble IASCOME statement.)

VI Ways of Worship

Here are four stories of Sunday mornings around the Anglican world. None of them is quite a documentary, and none is entirely imaginary. Each of them captures something of a local expression of Anglicanism. How do the people in the stories experience their Anglican identity in and around their liturgical celebrations? And how do we, when we read about these Anglican brothers and sisters, grow in our understanding of what it means for us to be part of the Anglican Communion?

1 Bernard Mizeki Anglican Church

Mary and Tsepo are going to Sunday church together. It's Bernard Mizeki Church, named after a local martyr, in the village where Mary lives and where Tsepo, her grandson, comes back to visit. (Tsepo works in the city, where he attends St. Francis' Anglican Church, Parkview).

The service starts at eight, but they arrive early because Mary helps to prepare the altar. The Churchwardens are there, unlocking everything. Mary collects the altar cloths and all the paraphernalia - candles, chalices and so on - and sets the altar. Tsepo is catching up on village news with one of the Churchwardens. People are trickling in. The priest hasn't arrived yet - he's on the road from somewhere else. This is the Sunday he comes to Bernard Mizeki.

There are no music books and no prayer books in the pews, but people who have books at home bring them along. As people arrive, singing starts: choruses, with bodies swaying. It won't be quiet, though, as people continue to arrive and greet each other. The men sit on the right hand side of the church, facing the altar, the women on the left. The Mothers' Union members are easily identified by their white tops and black skirts and Mothers' Union badges. Though Tsepo can sit with his girlfriend in the city church, he can't even sit with his grandmother in the village. The choir and the lay ministers are robing and heading for the room at the back. Hopefully by now the priest has arrived - they'd rather not start without him.

When the priest is robed and ready a signal is given and the chorus-singing stops. A hymn is announced from three different hymn books: English, isiXhosa and seTswana, all translations of *Ancient and Modern*. The singing starts, unaccompanied, and the ministers and the choir process in from the main entrance.

The priest and lay ministers lead the service from *An Anglican Prayer Book* in seTswana, and most of the people respond in seTswana, though the page numbers are the same for the English and isiXhosa versions of the book. The bible readings are taken from the Lectionary for the day, and are read in seTswana. A chorus is sung as the priest prepares to read the gospel. Although the church is small, the priest still carries the bible closer to the people for the gospel reading. Just before the sermon, the children go outside for Sunday School, where they are taught by teenagers and a couple of older people. They will come back in for their blessing at Communion time. The sermon is in seTswana, but is translated into isiXhosa by someone from the congregation or one of the lay ministers, complete with gestures imitated from the preacher. It could be quite a long sermon - the preacher hasn't been there for a month, and this is his big opportunity to teach the people.

The prayers are chosen from one of the four forms the Prayer Book offers,

Appendix

with more singing before and after the prayers. There are lots of local community concerns in the prayers: Mama Rose who's not well, the school books that need to arrive in time, the bishop who's coming to do confirmations in a fortnight, and the confirmation candidates. Tsepo notices that it will be the same bishop who visited Parkview a month or so back.

After the prayers, the notices are given: about the confirmation and the bishop's visit and the special meal to be held on that day, about money needed for flowers, and a reminder about Thursday's Mothers' Union meeting. Then there is the greeting of peace, and people are moving around everywhere with handshakes and hugs.

At the offertory, one of the Churchwardens puts the collection plate at the front, and people come singing and dancing down the aisle to make their offerings. Mama Mary and Tsepo, because he is visiting, bring up the bread and wine for the eucharist.

The priest sings the eucharistic Great Thanksgiving, with lots of gestures and signs of the cross. People sing the responses and the Lord's Prayer. The women come up first for Communion, though Tsepo's cousin, Patience, stays back with her baby. The men follow, then all the children come up for a blessing at the end of Communion.

Then there is more singing, a blessing and the dismissal, and a procession of all the ministers out of the church door. When the priest has said a final prayer with the lay ministers and the choir, the choir members go back into the church, still singing, to disrobe, while the priest greets the members of the congregation. Of course everyone has tea: the mothers go into the vestry to boil the kettle, set up tables outside, and bring out the cakes they have brought to share. Everyone is busy, catching up on news, drinking tea, paying funeral dues, asking Tsepo what he has been up to in the city.

2 St Mary's Anglican Church

Chris and Sophie arrive in plenty of time for High Mass, as it says on the notice board outside, at 11.00 am. On entering the church they notice the familiar smell of charcoal being lit for the incense. The notice board beside the door has posters advertising a big event at the Cathedral, and the forthcoming parish Pentecost pilgrimage.

Two congregation members are giving out hymn books and service booklets and a single sheet of paper with music and notices. The visitors take theirs and sit down at the back between a man in casual clothes and a woman with two young children. She is kneeling, holding a rosary in her hand, and the children are making sure they have all the same books as the adults, along with photocopied sheets with illustrations about the day's bible readings. Just to the side is a beautiful chapel with a statue of Mary holding the child Jesus, and several people are lighting candles on the stand in front of it. At the front of the church, three people in red cassocks and white cottas are setting up the chalices and lighting the candles in a highly ritualized way, bowing to the altar whenever they pass it.

At 11.00 am a bell sounds from the back and everyone stands as the organ plays the introduction to the hymn and everyone starts to sing as the choir and clergy process in, led by people carrying incense, cross and candles. People bow as the cross and priest pass. It all seems very dignified and formal. So far no announcement has been made, no words have been spoken, yet everyone seems to know what to expect and what to do. There are three clergy wearing matching vestments, and the priest presiding is a woman.

The words of the service are very familiar: 'Almighty God, to whom all hearts are open....' People are very comfortable with making gestures, standing and kneeling, and Chris and Sophie take their cues from the rest. They sit for the first reading, and a woman makes her way to the lectern carrying her own Bible. When she announces the reading and that she is using the Moffat translation, people smile as if they recognize a familiar eccentricity of hers. There is a splendid procession for the reading of the gospel. The priest preaches from the pulpit for 10 minutes, a challenging and humorous message based on the Gospel reading. After the Creed, which is sung, prayers of intercession are led by members of the congregation from the back of the church. There is plenty of silence, which Sophie and Chris use to add their own thoughts; and the prayers finish with the Hail Mary.

Then they stand up for the Peace, which the priest leads from the front. People turn only to their immediate neighbour with a handshake, and the children solemnly greet the visitors with just the right words. Another hymn

Appendix

starts without announcement and the sidespeople come round and take up the collection. Then a group of people process up to the altar carrying the wafer bread and wine. More incense is used, and the congregation is censed as well as the priest. All the servers seemed to know exactly what they are doing. The priest sings the first part of the Eucharistic Prayer and everyone responds. As the prayer progresses, bells are rung and there is an atmosphere of reverence and attentiveness in the church.

After the Lord's Prayer, which everyone sings, the sidespeople make sure the visitors know they are invited to the sanctuary for Communion. People genuflect, bow and cross themselves very unselfconsciously. The children receive communion too, carefully making the sign of the cross as they kneel. After Communion, back in their seats, there is quite a long silence and everyone seems very comfortable with it. Before the blessing, the priest invites everyone to a 'Refreshment Sunday Party' in the vicarage after the service, with canapés and pink champagne. Everyone stands to sing 'Guide me, O thou great Redeemer', which Chris thinks a bit rousing for Lent, and the choir and clergy process out again during a lively voluntary on the organ. The woman with the children escorts Sophie and Chris across to the vicarage for the party.

3 St Mark's Anglican Church

At 10.30 on Sunday morning, a crowd of university students have arrived at St Mark's for the main morning service. The notice board outside the building shows that there has already been an early morning service of Holy Communion here, according to the Book of Common Prayer of 1662, and there will be a youth service at 8.00 pm. There are little black books on shelves at the back of the church that have clearly been in use earlier in the day. The floor is carpeted and there are banners with scripture texts on them adorning the walls. Helpers are busy moving the chairs into a semi-circle from the earlier rows, so that everyone will be able to see the screen at the front. As people arrive they are given a leaflet with the week's coming events and prayer points, but for this service no books are needed.

Before the service, images of inner-city streetscapes and close-ups of children's faces are projected on the large screen, which soon comes into use for the words of the songs and some of the prayers. Towards the front of the building is a communion table that's not the centre of attention at present, as the music stands of the band are in front of it. The music will be provided by this group of very talented people who spent most of Saturday afternoon rehearsing. The music is loud, and while the words praise God, the musical idiom ranges from heavy rock to ballad style.

The service moves from a block of energetic and repetitive opening songs and choruses into a quieter mode, with prayers from a leader calling the congregation to be aware of God's presence and to prepare to hear God's word. It's all moving towards the centrepiece of the service: a substantial sermon. A good number of the congregation are checking references in their pew Bibles as the minister preaches. Some of the congregation seem to be taking notes. Key points and relevant scripture texts, and the occasional video clip, appear on the big screen as the sermon progresses. The sermon is part of a series looking at St Paul's letter to the Romans. After the sermon, there is plenty of time for unscripted prayer and testimony from a range of young adults. The shifts in focus are managed by another leader who may well be ordained, but who is wearing casual clothes like all the others present.

The prayers mention the local bishop, and the imminent visit of an African bishop who is being sponsored by the diocese to lead a local mission. In the notices, there is an appeal for additional prayer support for the family the parish has sent to run a children's home in Romania, and for accommodation that needs to be found locally for students from out of town.

After the service, there is excellent coffee, and an offer of pizza for those who want to stay and work on planning next week's service. There is a bookstall and Fair Trade craft stall, and someone is collecting signatures for a petition to cancel debt in the developing world.

4 St John's Anglican Church

In Japanese society, the Christian population is very small. Many Japanese people pay homage at a Shinto shrine, but only once a year, on New Year's Day. In such a society, it is not easy for many people to visit a

Appendix

Christian Church. For many, the distinction between Roman Catholic and Protestant churches is not clear. Still fewer people know about the Anglican Church. When people hear the name 'Nippon Sei Ko Kai - Anglican Church' they wonder whether it is Roman Catholic or Protestant. So an Anglican pastor or church member can only answer by saying, 'We are catholic, but not Roman Catholic. Please come and see. If you attend the Sunday service, you can find out.'

Akiko is a junior high school student. Her first impression is of the church building, and she is also attracted by the beautiful resonance of hymns and organ music. She has been standing outside the small country church, near the window, listening to the music flowing from inside. When she decides to enter the church and attend the Sunday 10.30 a.m. service, everything is a new experience for her. As she enters, she is impressed by the solemn, quiet atmosphere inside.

A church member who also stands near the door greets her. 'Hello, welcome. Is this your first time in a church?' An old man hands her three books, the Book of Common Prayer, a Hymnal, and the Lectionary for Year A, as well as a leaflet headed 'today's programme'. Akiko is a bit confused, but the old man kindly leads her to a seat and says, 'Please relax! People stand when they are singing, and sit to listen. They sometimes kneel when they pray. But please feel free to do as you wish.'

At 10.30, when the worship begins, people around her suddenly stand up and begin to sing. Ministers wearing unusual dress come in, and process to the front. During the service, everything is completely new to her. Sometimes she feels strange, because the ministers and people say prayers together, and act corporately.

After the service, the pastor introduces her to the congregation and says, 'Welcome to this church.' One lady - not so old - approaches Akiko, asks her impressions, and says, 'If you have time, please join us. We'll have lunch, it's Japanese noodles today.' Two or three young women, almost the same age as Akiko, also come up and welcome her and invite her to come along with them.

A few months have passed since Akiko's first visit. Now she participates in the church's Sunday service almost every week. Sometimes she can sit inside the church, very quietly. Little by little, she learns to pray, not only for herself, but for her family and friends and for people in distress. She has seen how, every Sunday, people pray for others who are ill and in trouble, and for peace for the world.

At the beginning, Akiko thought that religious faith was a very private matter, just for her personal rest and relief. But now she is gradually realizing that the Christian faith is not only an individual matter. Through the worship, and through encounters with members of the church, she now feels that she is accepted as a member of a family, the family of God. Akiko is beginning to think of being baptized, and belonging to the church formally. She thinks that she wants to share the bread and wine like the other members. She feels a kind of mystery is there. It is not easy to express, but she feels her life is strengthened by the mysterious power of God.

Suggestions for Study

Read the story. In a group, have someone read slowly aloud. Try to let your imagination visualize the events described. Take a few minutes to reflect on the story, letting it play in your mind. As you reflect on each story you might ask yourself the following questions, taking time to form your reply. In a group, members may first reflect in silence and then share their responses with each other, in smaller groups of five or six if there are many participants.

How much of the story reflects your own experience of worship?

Would you feel comfortable in this worship setting? If not, why not?

What elements in the story would you recognize as being particularly Anglican? What elements would be foreign to you as an Anglican?

Do the styles of worship reflected in these stories contribute to or detract from Anglican unity?

In the light of these stories what would you seek to change in your own pattern of worship?

The four vignettes were intended to illustrate the diversity of worship in the Anglican Communion. Please write a description of Anglican worship which would express the hope of our calling to be 'one in Christ'.